Did CAVEMEN BRUSH THEIR TEETH?

This edition published in 2024 by Arcturus Publishing Limited
26/27 Bickels Yard, 151–153 Bermondsey Street,
London SE1 3HA

Illustrator: Luke Séguin-Magee
Author: Anne Rooney
Editors: William Potter and Violet Peto
Designer: Steve Flight

CH007050NT
Supplier: 10, Date 1023, PI 00005516

Printed in the UK

MIX
Paper from
responsible sources
FSC® C018072
www.fsc.org

CONTENTS

ICKY BODIES 5

FOUL FOOD 27

APPALLING ANIMALS 49

HORRID HISTORY 79

SCARY SCIENCE 111

PASS THE BUCKET

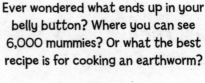

Ever wondered what ends up in your belly button? Where you can see 6,000 mummies? Or what the best recipe is for cooking an earthworm?

The answers to these and many other icky and puzzling questions on history, science, and the human body can be found in this book. Some are so gross they are dangerous, and people have spent years training themselves to do them. So don't try any of them at home—leave it to the experts!

ICKY BODIES

WHAT HAPPENS TO YOUR DEAD SKIN?

Dust mites are found in all houses. They eat the dead skin we shed all the time and live in beds, carpets, rugs, and anywhere else snug that collects flakes of skin. Ten billion scales of skin fall off your body every day, so there's plenty for them to feed on!

HOW BIG IS YOUR SKIN?

The skin of an adult laid out flat on the floor would cover about 18 square ft (1.67 square m).

DID YOU KNOW?

You shed and regrow your skin roughly every 27 days, making a total of about 1,000 complete skins in a lifetime. A person who lives to 70 years of age will shed 47.6 kg (105 lb) of skin.

WHY IS A BRUISE PURPLE?

A bruise is bleeding under your skin. The blood can't get out if there isn't a cut, so it just leaks around—it's purple because that's the hue of blood that doesn't have any oxygen in it.

WHAT CAUSES HEAT RASH?

Prickly heat rash is caused by sweat sticking to the layer of dead skin cells on top of your skin. Since the cells can't fall off, the sweat can't escape and makes the live cells underneath swell up.

WHY DO YOU TURN PALE WHEN FRIGHTENED?

You turn white when you're really scared because blood drains from your skin. This protected primitive humans from bleeding to death if bitten by scary, wild animals.

HOW MUCH BLOOD DOES YOUR HEART PUMP?

About 70 ml (2.5 fluid ounces) of blood are spurted out of your heart with each beat.

WHAT'S INSIDE A DROP OF BLOOD?

A single drop of blood contains 250 million blood cells.

DID YOU KNOW?

For a work entitled Self, created in 1991, English sculptor Marc Quinn made a copy of his head, formed from his own deep-frozen blood. Quinn collected almost 4 l (8 pints) of his blood over five months, poured it into the form of his head, and froze it.

WHAT HAPPENS IF YOU DON'T BRUSH YOUR TEETH?

If you don't brush plaque off your teeth, it hardens into a substance called tartar, which is like cement and impossible to remove with your toothbrush.

DID CAVEMEN BRUSH THEIR TEETH?

Toothbrushes date back to the Ancient Egyptians. Before that, our ancestors probably used to pick their teeth with sticks.

WHAT DID PEOPLE DO BEFORE DENTISTS INVENTED FILLINGS?

Long ago, rich people used to pay for teeth to be pulled from poor people—often teenagers—and implanted in their own jaws when their rotten teeth were removed.

WHAT IS LIPOSUCTION?

Liposuction is a popular operation in Europe and the USA among people who feel they are too fat. A surgeon sticks a long, hollow needle into the fat part—such as the tummy or thighs—uses ultrasound to turn the fat to yellow mush, and then sucks it out through the needle.

HOW CAN YOU REMOVE WRINKLES?

A facelift to remove wrinkles involves cutting away part of the skin, pulling the remainder tight again, and stitching it in place. Some people have injections of collagen to "plump up" their wrinkles. The collagen—a material found in skin—is usually taken from pigs or cows.

IS ATHLETE'S FOOT A SPORTS INJURY?

Athlete's foot is a fungus that grows in the warm, sweaty spaces between your toes. It causes itching and cracked skin.

HOW MANY HAIRS DO YOU HAVE?

An adult has around five million hairs on his or her head and body.

WHICH HAIRS GROW THE FASTEST?

Beards grow faster than any other body hair. If a man never cut his beard, it would grow 9.1 m (30 ft) in his lifetime.

HOW MANY HAIRS DO YOU LOSE IN A DAY?

You lose 80 hairs from your head every day—but you have about 100,000, so don't worry, you won't start to look bald just yet. And they regrow quickly when you're young.

DO BALD PEOPLE HAVE ANY HAIR?

Yes! Even bald people have very fine hair—called vellus—on their head.

HOW POWERFUL IS YOUR STOMACH ACID?

The acid in your stomach is so strong that it can dissolve steel razor blades—it's still not a good idea to eat them, though!

WHY DOES YOUR TUMMY SOMETIMES MAKE NOISES?

Stomach gurgling—called borborygmus by scientists—is the sound of half-digested food, gas, and stomach acid churning around.

WHY DO YOU BURP AND FART?

Air you swallow and gas released from food as you digest it comes out as a burp or a fart—which one depends on how far through your intestines it has gone.

WHICH FOODS MAKE YOU FART

Foods that will make you fart include beans, bran, broccoli, cabbage, cauliflower, and onions.

WHY CAN A FART SMELL BAD?

A smelly fart contains the same gas that makes rotten eggs stink—hydrogen sulfide.

WHY DO SOME PEOPLE SCAR THEIR SKIN ON PURPOSE?

In some parts of Africa and on some Pacific islands, people make patterns of raised scars on their skin as a decoration or to show their bravery. The wounds are made with sharp spikes or thorns from plants and often rubbed with special kinds of earth or leaves to created tattoos.

WHY DO SURMA GIRLS STRETCH THEIR LIPS?

Surma girls of Ethiopia put clay plates in their lower lip, stretching the lip outward. The size of the plate indicates how many cattle a man needs to provide to marry the girl—they can be up to 15 cm (6 inches) across.

DO SOME WOMEN WEAR METAL RINGS TO STRETCH THEIR NECKS?

The women of the Karen tribe in Thailand traditionally wear masses of metal bands around their necks. The first bands are added on a girl's fifth birthday, and more are added every few months. If the bands are removed, the woman's weakened neck can't support her head. Removing the bands has become an effective punishment.

DO SOME PEOPLE KEEP A BABY'S UMBILICAL CORD?

In some countries, the umbilical cord—the cord that attaches the unborn baby to its mother—is dried and kept after birth to use in spells or medicines.

DID YOU KNOW?

Different cultures practice different traditions all over the world. Some of these might seem weird to you, but don't forget that **your** cultural practices may seem weird to other cultures!

WHAT IS THE MOST COMMON PARASITIC WORM IN HUMANS?

The maw-worm or large roundworm is a parasitic worm that infects about one-sixth of the human race. It can grow to 30 cm (1 foot). It can leave your body through any gap or hole, including the corner of the eye.

WHAT IS A HOOKWORM?

At least 1.3 billion people are infected with a small hookworm that attaches to the inside of the gut. A lot of attached hookworms look like fur or a thick carpet. Around the world, they suck a total of around 10 million l (21 million pints) of blood a day.

WHERE DO TAPEWORMS LIVE?

The larvae of the pork tapeworm, hatched from eggs eaten in infected pork, can travel around the body and live in the brain, eyes, heart, or muscles.

HOW LONG CAN A TAPEWORM GROW?

A beef tapeworm, caught from eating eggs in infected beef, can grow to 12 m (39 ft) long in the human gut.
The longest tapeworm ever found in a human was around 33 m (108 ft) long.

DID YOU KNOW?

At any one time, parasites account for 1/100th of your body weight.

HOW MUCH PEE DO YOU PRODUCE?

On average, you will produce about 511 l (135 gallons) of urine in a year—enough to fill two bathtubs!

IS PEE USEFUL FOR ANYTHING?

Urine is a good remedy for jellyfish stings, so if you're standing in the sea and get stung, just pee down your legs. Ancient Romans used to brush their teeth with urine, and it was used as a mouthwash until the 1800s in Europe.

CAN YOU DRINK YOUR OWN PEE?

Urine doesn't contain bacteria. Shipwrecked sailors used to drink it with no ill effects.

DID YOU KNOW?

A newborn baby produces its own body weight in poop every 60 hours.

HOW MUCH OF THE FOOD YOU EAT TURNS TO POOP?

Your body absorbs about two-thirds of the volume of the food you eat—the rest is squished into poop.

HOW LONG DOES IT TAKE FOR FOOD TO TURN INTO POOP?

It can take up to two days for food to pass through your body—from going in your mouth to coming out your rear.

WHY DOES POOP SMELL?

Poop smells largely because the microbes in your gut produce two stinky chemicals as they work to break down your food—indole and skatole.

DID YOU KNOW?

The toilet paper that Americans use in one day would go around the world nine times.

HOW MUCH SALIVA DO YOU PRODUCE IN A DAY?

A person produces 1.5 l (2.6 pints) of spit (saliva) every day and swallows almost all of it.

WHAT IS PUS?

When a wound gets infected, it oozes yellow pus. Pus is a mixture of dead blood cells, bacteria, and other dead cells from your body.

WHAT ENDS UP IN YOUR BELLY BUTTON?

Your belly button is formed from the shriveled up stump of the umbilical cord—the tube that connected you to your mother's body before you were born. The stuff that collects in your belly button is a mix of dirt, dead skin cells, and oils from your body.

HOW IS EARWAX MADE?

The medical name for earwax is cerumen; it is produced by glands to protect you from getting dirt, dust, and germs deep in your ear. The wax slowly hardens and comes to the edge of your ear to fall out. If it doesn't fall out, it can harden into a plug of wax up to about 2.5 cm (1 inch) long.

WHAT HAPPENS IF MY EAR GETS FULL OF EARWAX?

If too much wax builds up in your ears, a doctor can soften it and then scoop it out with a special spoon called a curette.

DID YOU KNOW?

People who live in big cities make more earwax than those who live in the country, where the air is cleaner.

WHAT IS SNOT MADE OF?

Nose pickings are a mix of drying mucus and rubbish filtered out of the air you breathe in—pollen, dust, smoke, dirt, sand, and even tiny particles of dust from space!

HOW MUCH MUCUS DO YOU SWALLOW?

You swallow over 1 l (2 pints) of mucus (snot) every day.

DID YOU KNOW?

Rhinotillexomania is the scientific word for picking your nose.

HOW MANY TEARS DO YOU CRY?

Your eyes make 4.5 l (8 pints) of tears a year—they keep your eyes wet even if you're not crying.

WHY DO YOU WAKE UP WITH GUNK IN YOUR EYES?

When you sleep, you aren't blinking, so there's no way to sweep away the mix of water, oils, and other chemicals that wash over your eyes. Instead, they dry out around the edges of your eyes, making crunchy or slimy yellow gunk.

HOW MUCH DO YOU SWEAT IN A DAY?

Adult feet produce about a quarter of a cup of sweat a day from 250,000 pores—wait four days, and you could make a cup of foot-sweat tea!

WHY DOES SWEAT SMELL BAD?

Sweat doesn't actually smell—it's the bacteria breaking it down that produce the stink.

DID YOU KNOW?

Right-handed people sweat most under their right arm; left-handed people sweat most under their left arm.

HOW FAST IS A S...

When you breathe normally, air goes into y...
6.5 km (4 miles) per hour. When you take a...
something, it goes in at 32 km (20 miles) per hou...
sneeze, it comes out at 160 km (100 miles) per...

DO SNEEZES SPREAD GERMS?

When you sneeze, up to a million tiny viruses are sprayed out of your nose and mouth. Just one of these can be enough to infect someone else.

HOW FAR CAN YOU THROW UP?

The best recorded distance for projectile vomiting is 8 m (27 ft)!

WHAT HAPPENS IF YOU VOMIT WITH YOUR MOUTH CLOSED?

If you try to stop yourself from throwing up by closing your mouth, the vomit will just come out of your nose.

DO YOUR FINGERNAILS AND HAIR KEEP GROWING AFTER YOU DIE?

No, but it can appear so! Your body starts to dry out and shrink, creating the illusion that your hair and nails are still growing after death.

CAN YOU STILL THINK IF YOUR HEAD IS CHOPPED OFF?

If your head is chopped off, you can remain conscious for about 25 seconds!

DID YOU KNOW?

To save space, 98 percent of dead Japanese people are cremated rather than buried. The weight of ashes from the average cremated human body is 4 kg (9 lb).

FOUL
FOOD

HOW MUCH FOOD DO YOU EAT IN A LIFETIME?

An average person eats around 22,700 kg (50,000 lb) of food over the course of his or her life.

WHAT DID THE ROMANS FEAST ON?

Roman banquets often featured hummingbirds cooked in walnut shells and roasted stuffed dormice, sometimes rolled in honey and poppy seeds. The Romans even had farms producing dormice because they were so popular. Once, at a Roman banquet, a slave stabbed the stomach of a roast boar to release a flock of live thrushes.

DID YOU KNOW?

In 1135, King Henry I of England died from eating too many lampreys—a kind of eel that sucks its victims to death.

DID YOU KNOW?

In the 1800s, it was common to mix ground bones into flour to make it go further.

28

DO PEOPLE REALLY DRINK BLOOD?

Blood soup is popular in many parts of the world. In Poland, people eat a duck-blood soup called czarnina; in Korea, pig-blood curd soup is called seonjiguk; and in the Philippines, people eat a pig-blood stew called dinuguan. In the Massai Mara in Africa, people drink blood drained from the neck of a live cattle with a straw, mixed with milk.

ARE COW EYES A DELICACY?

In France, calves' eyes are soaked in water, then boiled and stuffed and finally, deep-fried in bread crumbs.

CAN YOU SWALLOW A TONGUE?

Cow's tongue is often sold with the salivary glands—the parts that make spit—ready for boiling. The tongue can weigh up to 2.3 kg (5 lb).

WHAT IS HAGGIS?

The Scottish dish haggis is made by cutting up the heart, lungs, liver, and small intestine of a calf or sheep and cooking it with suet (the fat from the animal's kidneys), oatmeal, onions, and herbs in the animal's stomach.

WHAT IS HEADCHEESE?

An American delicacy called headcheese, similar to British brawn, is made by cooking a whole cow or pig head into a mush and letting it cool into a jellylike mass.

DID YOU KNOW?

When a pig is roasted in Cuba, the skull is cracked open, and each guest takes a spoon to share scoops of brain.

WHAT'S THE TASTIEST PART OF A LOBSTER?

Slimy green stuff that looks like mucus is supposedly the best part of a lobster or crayfish. It's found in the head. Some Americans eat the main part of the lobster meat and then suck the head to get the gunk out.

CAN EATING FISH KILL YOU?

In Japan, the blowfish is a delicacy, even though it contains a poison gland that, if not properly removed, kills anyone who eats it.

DID YOU KNOW?

In Hong Kong, you can buy bags of crispy fried crabs as a snack.

WHAT'S THE SMELLIEST SEAFOOD?

At the winter festival of Thorrablot, Icelanders eat hákarl—rotten shark. Shark meat is buried in the ground for six to eight weeks then dried in the open air for two months.

WHAT ABOUT STINK HEADS?

Stink heads are a traditional Alaskan dish. Fish heads—often from salmon—are buried in pits lined with moss for a few weeks or months until rotten. They are then kneaded like pastry to mix up all the parts and eaten.

DID YOU KNOW?

In Newfoundland, Canada, seal-flipper pie is a traditional dish for the end of a seal hunt.

ARE DRUNKEN SHRIMPS REALLY DRUNK?

Drunken shrimp, served in China, are live shrimp swimming in a bowl of rice wine. The idea is to catch them with chopsticks and bite the heads off.

WHAT DOES SHARK-FIN SOUP TASTE LIKE?

In China, shark-fin soup is made from the salted, sun-dried fins of sharks. It is like a bowl of glue since the fin contains a lot of gelatin.

DID YOU KNOW?

A traditional dish in London is eels boiled and served cold in gelatin.

DO PEOPLE EAT FISH EYES?

In the Philippines, the eyes are considered the tastiest part of a steamed fish. Suck out the gloop and spit out the hard cornea.

DID YOU KNOW?

The Korean delicacy sannakji consists of still-wriggling slices of octopus tentacle.

IS SEA CUCUMBER A VEGETABLE?

In the Samoan Islands, the intestines of sea cucumbers are steeped in seawater and sold in jars. The sea cucumber is a slithery, tubelike animal and not a cucumber at all. When it's cooked, it's called a sea slug.

CAN YOU EAT CHICKEN FEET?

Crispy fried duck or chicken feet are a delicacy in China. In the United States, whole chicken feet are sometimes pickled or made into soup.

DO EGGS SOMETIMES HAVE LIVE CHICKS INSIDE?

In the Philippines, fertilized duck or chicken eggs are cooked and eaten—with the unhatched chick partly grown inside. It's called balut, in case you want to avoid it on the menu.

DID YOU KNOW?

In the Faroe Islands, to the north of the UK, a popular dish is puffin stuffed with rhubarb.

IS BIRD'S NEST SOUP REALLY MADE FROM NESTS?

Bird's nest soup is a delicacy in China. It's made from the nests of a special variety of swift that builds its nest from dried strands of its own spit. The nest is soaked in water to soften it, then any sticks and feathers are removed before it is made into a gluey, sticky soup.

ARE ANY TRADITIONAL FOODS NOW BANNED?

Until 1999, it was legal to enjoy ortolan in France—a tiny, rare, songbird, fattened in a dark box to three times its normal size, then drowned in brandy and spit roasted for a few minutes before being eaten whole, innards included. (It was okay to leave the head and beak.) Traditionally, it was eaten with a napkin draped over your head and the plate, so that none of the delicious smell could escape.

DID YOU KNOW?

In Hungary, scrambled eggs are fried up with the blood from a freshly slaughtered pig.

HOW DO YOU EAT SQUIRREL BRAINS?

In the southern United States, squirrel brains are cooked still in the head. You then crack the skull and scoop the brains out with your fingers and a fork.

HOW DO COOK A HEDGEHOG?

Romany people in Europe and poor peasants used to cook wild hedgehogs by rolling them in mud and baking them in the embers of a fire. When the mud dries, the spines can be peeled off with the mud.

DID YOU KNOW?

Some Arctic explorers have been poisoned by eating polar bear liver. The polar bear eats so much fish that fatal levels of vitamin D collect in its liver.

WHAT TREATS CAN I TASTE IN TEXAS?

In Texas, USA, there's an annual rattlesnake roundup. What to do with all the rattlesnakes? Skin them, gut them, cut them into chunks, cover in batter, and deep-fry. They also eat armadillos in Texas, roasted in their shells and stuffed with carrots, apples, and potatoes.

IS IT TRUE SOME PEOPLE DRINK SNAKE BLOOD?

In Vietnam, cobra hearts are a common snack. They can be eaten raw, even still beating, with a small glass of cobra blood or dropped into a glass of rice wine. The kidney is often included as an extra tidbit. Snake wine in China is a very potent alcoholic drink spiced with juice from the gallbladder of a live snake.

DID YOU KNOW?

In Ecuador, a family barbecue can include guinea pig and snake kebabs.

WHAT'S THE STICKIEST FOOD?

Ambuyat, eaten in Brunei, is made from pulp from the sago palm stewed in water for several hours. The same mixture is made to stick the roof on a house! The sago worm, which lives inside rotting sago palms, is often cooked and eaten.

WHAT'S A REALLY WILD FEAST?

In the 1800s, naturalist Frank Buckland served meals such as mice on toast, roasted parrots, and stewed sea slug. He tried to make soup from an elephant's trunk, but even after several days' cooking, it was still too chewy.

DID YOU KNOW?

In Indonesia, deep-fried monkey toes are eaten by sucking the meat straight off the bone.

Biltong is enjoyed as a snack by rugby fans in South Africa. It's dried strips of any meat, such as elephant, eland, or antelope.

CAN YOU EAT BATS?

In Palau, an island in the western Pacific Ocean, whole fruit bats, complete with skin, may be ordered as a starter or main course.

DID YOU KNOW?

In Mongolia, camel or horse milk is stored in a cleaned horse stomach or hide bag and hung up in the ger (tent). Everyone who passes the door has to stir or hit the bag. It slowly ferments into a slightly alcoholic, cheesy yogurt drink that everyone drinks, even children.

IS THERE A RESTAURANT THAT SERVES BUGS?

The Insect Club, a restaurant in the United States, serves only dishes made with insects. The menu includes cricket pizza, insect chocolates, and "insects in a blanket"——crickets, mealworms, and blue cheese in puff pastry.

DID YOU KNOW?

In India, ants are roasted, ground to a paste, and served as chutney.

HOW DO YOU EAT AN ANT?

In northern Australia, children often eat green ants. Pick them up, squish the head so they don't nibble you, and bite off the body.

WHAT'S BETTER THAN POPCORN IN COLOMBIA?

At the movies in Colombia, you can snack on paper cones filled with giant fried or toasted ants.

WHAT'S THE BEST RECIPE FOR AN EARTHWORM?

An international contest to find the best recipe for cooking earthworms included entries of stews, salads, and soups but was won by a recipe for applesauce-surprise cake. Guess what the surprise was!

DID YOU KNOW?

In Sardinia, cheese is left in the sun for flies to lay their eggs in. When the maggots hatch, the swarming mass is spread on bread and eaten.

HOW IS HONEY MADE?

Honey is bee vomit. Bees drink nectar from flowers, which they turn into honey before throwing it back up to store in the hive.

DID YOU KNOW?

Honey found in ancient Egyptian tombs has been tasted by archaeologists and found to be still edible, after thousands of years.

COULD YOU SURVIVE ON BUGS?

The Air Force Survival Manual issued to US airmen explains which bugs to eat in an emergency for maximum taste and nutrition. US Air Force pilot Captain Scott O'Grady was shot down over Bosnia in 1995 and survived for six days eating only ants.

DO PEOPLE REALLY EAT SPIDERS?

In Cambodia, giant grilled spiders are a popular street snack.

DID YOU KNOW?

In France, over 40,000 metric tons (88 million lb) of snails are consumed every year.

WHAT IS A GLUTTON?

A glutton is a greedy eater. The Roman emperor Nero kept a "glutton"—an Egyptian slave who ate everything he was given to eat, including human flesh.

DID THE AZTECS EAT PEOPLE?

The Aztecs gave people who were to be human sacrifices many last meals—they fattened them up for up to a year. They didn't eat the sacrifices, but they did have a dish called tlacatalalli, which was a stew made from corn and human beings.

DID YOU KNOW?

Some Amazonian tribes used to make a soup with the ground bones of their dead relatives.

WHAT'S THE ODDEST CHOICE OF ICE CREAM?

Choices of ice cream available in Japan include octopus, cactus, chicken wing, and crab. A restaurant in Osaka, Japan, serves whale ice cream made from the blubber of the minke whale.

WHAT'S THE SMELLIEST FRUIT YOU CAN EAT?

Durian is a fruit the size of a soccer ball, covered in spikes, which smells like rotting meat. It's banned from flights, because of the smell but it's supposed to taste good, though!

DID YOU KNOW?

Tradition tells that the French cheese Roquefort was discovered when a shepherd abandoned his lunch in a cave to chase a pretty girl he saw outside. When he came back months later, the cheese had started to get rotten but still tasted good.

WHAT'S THE BIGGEST BURGER YOU CAN EAT?

A restaurant in Pennsylvania offers a hamburger that weighs 4 kg (9 lb). No one has yet managed to finish one.

COULD YOU RECOMMEND AN UNUSUAL WINE?

Baby-mouse wine, from China, is a bottle of wine packed with baby mice to add taste. Spider wine, from Cambodia, is actually rice wine—the spiders are added later. Eskimos have been known to make seagull wine—put a seagull in a bottle of water, wait for it to go bad—drink!

DID YOU KNOW?

The alcoholic drink mescal has a cactus maggot preserved in the bottle.

WHAT'S THE MOST-EXPENSIVE OMELET?

An omelet costing $1,000 and called the Zillion Dollar Lobster Frittata was sold by a restaurant in New York. It contains a whole lobster and 280 kg (10 ounces) of caviar, as well as eggs, cream, potato, and whiskey.

DO PEOPLE IN SPAIN FIGHT WITH TOMATOES?

The town of Bunol, in Spain, has an annual tomato fight, when up to 25,000 people throw around 100 metric tons (220,000 lb) of tomatoes at each other. The streets can be flooded up to 30 cm (12 inches) deep with juice.

DID YOU KNOW?

In 1973, a Swedish candy salesman was buried in a coffin made of chocolate.

APPALLING ANIMALS

HOW MUCH DOES AN ELEPHANT POOP?

An elephant produces 23 kg (50 lb) of poop every day.

HOW THICK IS A HIPPO'S SKIN?

The skin of a hippopotamus measures about 4 cm (1.5 inches) thick. That's 2.5 cm (over 1 inch) thicker than human skin.

CAN ANIMALS EAT TOO MUCH?

The banded tenrec, a kind of hedgehog from Madagascar, sometimes eats so many worms, bugs, and slugs that it makes itself sick.

WHY ARE COWS ALWAYS CHEWING?

Cows partly digest the grass they eat, then vomit it back up into their mouths and chew and swallow it all over again. That's what they're doing when you see them chewing in a field when they're not munching on a fresh mouthful of grass.

HOW DOES BLOOD REACH A GIRAFFE'S HEAD?

A giraffe has special valves in its arteries, so that its blood can reach its head. Without them, it would need a heart as big as its whole body!

DID YOU KNOW?

A giraffe can lick inside its own ears.

WHAT IS A KING RAT?

Rats that hibernate together sometimes get their tails tied up in a knot. If they pee over themselves in the winter, they can freeze together in a block. A knot of rats is called a king rat.

DO RABBITS EAT THEIR OWN POOP?

Rabbits partially digest the grass they eat and then excrete it as soft, gluey pellets. They then eat these to finish digesting their meal properly.

DOES CAT PEE GLOW IN THE DARK?

Yes, but it has to be very dark, if you're thinking of testing it.

DID YOU KNOW?

Three-toed sloths move so slowly that algae often grows on their fur.

CAN BAT POOP BE USED AS FERTILIZER?

Bracken Cave in Texas is home to 20 million bats. The floor is caked in a thick layer of bat droppings. Bat poop lies so deep on the floors of some bat caves that people harvest it to sell as fertilizer for plants.

HOW MANY BUGS DOES A BAT CATCH IN A NIGHT?

A single bat can eat 3,000 to 7,000 mosquitoes in a single night; a colony of 500 bats goes through a quarter of a million bugs an hour.

DO VAMPIRE BATS SUCK BLOOD?

Vampire bats don't suck—they make a cut in their victim, then lick the blood as it flows out. To keep it flowing, they have an anticoagulant in their spit—a chemical that keeps blood from clotting and forming a scab.

DO OPOSSUMS REALLY PLAY DEAD?

Yes. When an opossum is threatened, it plays dead—it lies still, its tongue hanging out, poops on itself, and oozes green slime that smells of rotting flesh.

DO ECHIDNAS HAVE POUCHES?

The echidna is a mammal that lays an egg and keeps it in a pouch on its stomach. The pouch grows just before the female produces the egg and disappears again after the baby has left it.

DID YOU KNOW?

The armadillo produces so much spit that it has a special reservoir to store it in.

WHY DO OWLS TURN THEIR HEADS TO FACE BACKWARD?

Owl eyes are too large to move in their eye sockets, so owls have developed the ability to turn their heads around farther than other birds can.

DO ANY BIRDS EAT TOO MUCH TO FLY?

Vultures gorging themselves on a carcass sometimes eat so much that they can't fly. They then vomit to make themselves lighter.

HOW DID THE BUTCHER BIRD GET ITS NAME?

The butcher bird (shrike) impales mice, small birds, and lizards on spikes to hold them still while it eats them.

DID YOU KNOW?

A baby robin eats 4 m (14 ft) of earthworms a day!

HOW DO SHARKS FIND THEIR PREY?

Sharks have special organs in their snouts and elsewhere that let them detect the electric fields produced by living animals. They can then home in on the animals to eat them. A shark can taste blood over 1 km (half a mile) away.

ARE BABY TIGER SHARKS DANGEROUS?

The embryos of tiger sharks fight each other in the womb, the strongest killing and eating the others, so that only one is ever born.

DID YOU KNOW?

A stingray has a special cap on the end of its tail that breaks off when it stings, allowing poison to pour out into the wound it's made in its victim.

WHICH SEA CREATURE HAS THE LARGEST EYES?

The vampire squid has the largest eyes of any animal for its body size. The squid is 28 cm (11 inches) long, and its eyes are 2.5 cm (1 inch) across. The equivalent would be a person with eyes the size of ping-pong paddles!

ARE THERE ANY ANIMALS WITH JUST ONE EYE?

Copepods are tiny crustaceans that swim around in groups of up to a trillion. They are the only known creature that has just one eye.

DID YOU KNOW?

When a fish called the Pacific grenadier is pulled out of the sea by fishermen, the change in pressure makes gas inside it expand quickly and its stomach pops out of its mouth.

HOW DOES A VIPER CLOSE ITS MOUTH?

The viperfish has teeth so long, it can't close its mouth and has to open its jaws out flat before it can swallow. Its teeth are half the length of its head!

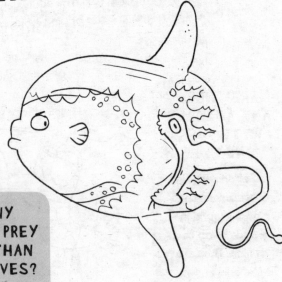

CAN ANY FISH EAT PREY BIGGER THAN THEMSELVES?

The deep-sea gulper eel can eat fish larger than itself. It can open its mouth so wide that its jaw bends back on itself at an angle of more than 180 degrees.

DID YOU KNOW?

In some types of anglerfish, the male is much smaller than the female and attaches himself to her body for life. After a while, he becomes fused to her and their body systems combine. His only role is to fertilize her eggs, and he is nourished by her blood.

WHERE DO PEARL FISH SLEEP BY DAY?

The pearl fish swims into a sea cucumber's anus and lives inside it during the day, coming out at night. The sea cucumber breathes through its bottom, so it can't keep the fish out!

CAN ELECTRIC EELS REALLY SHOCK YOU?

Electric eels can deliver a shock of 500 volts to stun their dinner into submission.

HOW DO FISH SPOT FOOD IN THE DARKEST DEPTHS?

The anglerfish has a glowing blob attached to a spike at the front of its head. In the dark, deep sea, the glowing blob attracts small prey, which the anglerfish then sucks in and gobbles up.

WHAT'S THE YUCKIEST FISH FEEDER?

The slime eel, or hagfish, feeds on dead and dying fish at the bottom of the sea. It goes into its victim through the mouth or eye socket and eats it away from the inside, leaving only a bag of skin and bones.

DID YOU KNOW?

A jellyfish excretes its poop through its mouth—it has only one opening and uses it for all purposes.

CAN OCTOPUSES SQUEEZE THROUGH SMALL HOLES?

An octopus has to turn itself inside out to eat, since its mouth is hidden in between its tentacles. A 32 kg (70 lb) octopus can squeeze through a hole the size of a tennis ball.

ARE KOMODO DRAGONS POISONOUS?

Komodo dragons are lizards 3 m (10 ft) long. They aren't poisonous, but there are so many bacteria in their mouths—growing in rotten meat between their teeth—that a bite from one often leads to blood poisoning and death. Baby Komodo dragons will eat their brothers and sisters if they are hungry and there is no other food.

DID YOU KNOW?

The gavial, a kind of crocodile from India, has over 100 teeth.

HOW DO YOU STOP A GILA MONSTER?

The Gila monster is a lizard from South America and Mexico. Although it's only about 0.5 m (2 ft) long, its bite is so strong that the only way to detach one that's bitten you is to drown it.

WERE THERE REALLY CROCODILES AT THE TIME OF THE DINOSAURS?

Over 100 million years ago, crocodiles were twice the size they are now—up to 12 m (40 ft) long—and could eat dinosaurs.

DO CROCODILES CHEW?

Crocodiles can't bite and chew. Instead, they hold their prey underwater to drown it, then twist their bodies around to tear chunks off the victim.

DID YOU KNOW?

Crocodiles carry their young around in their mouths.

WHAT'S THE WORLD'S DEADLIEST SNAKE?

The carpet viper kills more people in the world than any other type of snake. Its bite leads to uncontrollable bleeding.

WHAT MAKES THE RATTLE ON A RATTLESNAKE?

The rattle on a rattlesnake's tail is made of rings of dead skin. It builds up as the snake grows older, so the louder the rattle, the larger the snake.

DID YOU KNOW?

A full-grown python can swallow a pig whole.

HOW LONG IS A CHAMELEON'S TONGUE?

A chameleon's tongue can be twice as long as its body and must be kept curled up to fit inside its mouth. The end of its tongue can have a club-like lump oiled with sticky goo, which helps it catch insects.

CAN A CHAMELEON LOOK TWO WAYS AT ONCE?

The eyes of a chameleon can move separately, so it can look in two directions at once.

DID YOU KNOW?

The horned lizard from South America shoots blood out of its eyes when it's attacked. It increases the blood pressure in its sinuses until they explode, spraying blood onto the attacker.

IS THERE REALLY A SEE-THROUGH FROG?

The glass frog has a transparent body—its blood vessels, stomach, and beating heart are all visible.

DO GECKOS HAVE EYELIDS?

Some geckos have no eyelids—they lick their eyeballs to clean them!

DID YOU KNOW?

The axolotl is a pale amphibian that is partway between a tadpole and a lizard and lives in a single lake in Mexico. Some axolotls change shape and become land creatures, but most don't ever change.

CAN FROGS SURVIVE FREEZING?

The wood frog that lives in the Arctic Circle can stay deep-frozen for weeks and survive.

DO TOADS GET SICK?

When a toad is sick, it vomits up its own stomach, which hangs out of its mouth for a short time before it swallows it back down.

DID YOU KNOW?

The African clawed toad lays up to 10,000 eggs, but many of its tadpoles are deformed. The parents eat the deformed ones when they hatch.

DID YOU KNOW?

The babies of the Surinam toad grow under the mother's skin on her back. They stay there for up to 130 days.

WHAT'S THE WORLD'S BIGGEST SPIDER?

Goliath birdeater spiders are the world's largest spider by mass. They can grow to the size of a dinner plate and kill small birds.

HOW DO SPIDERS FEED?

Spiders inject flies and bugs with a chemical that paralyzes them and dissolves their insides. The spider then sucks out the liquid since it can't chew. A spider that isn't hungry will wrap up extra bugs in its web to keep for later.

DO SPIDERS EAT OTHER SPIDERS?

The female black widow spider eats the male after mating, sometimes eating up to 25 partners a day. Now that's a man-eater!

HOW TOUGH IS A SCORPION?

A scorpion can go for a whole year without eating. It can withstand extremes of temperature and even radiation. A scorpion could be frozen in a block of ice for three weeks and walk away unharmed. It can survive 200 times the dose of radiation that would kill a person!

DID YOU KNOW?

A pregnant scorpion will sometimes reabsorb its babies instead of giving birth to them.

DO SCORPIONS GLOW IN THE DARK?

Yes, but you need ultraviolet light to see them.

DO ALL MOSQUITOES BITE?

Only female mosquitoes bite and suck blood—they need the protein in blood, so that they can lay eggs. The males eat only nectar from flowers.

HOW MUCH BLOOD DOES A MOSQUITO DRINK?

A mosquito can drink one-and-a-half times its own weight in blood at a single meal.

DID YOU KNOW?

Mosquitoes in the Arctic hatch when the snows thaw, sometimes making such large swarms that they blot out the sun.

HOW TOUGH ARE COCKROACHES?

A cockroach can withstand more than 120 times the force of Earth's gravity—an astronaut passes out at 12 times the pressure of gravity. A cockroach can also survive being frozen in a block of ice for two days and even live for a week after its head is cut off!

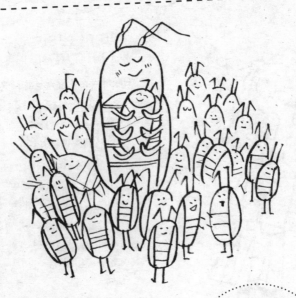

HOW FAST DO COCKROACHES BREED?

Cockroaches breed so fast that if all the young survived and reproduced, there would be 10 million cockroaches from a single pair by the end of a year.

DID YOU KNOW?

Cockroaches taste through their feet.

HOW DO FLIES EAT?

Flies eat by vomiting up something they've eaten previously, so that the chemicals in their vomit can start to dissolve the new meal. When it's sloppy, they suck it all up again. That's why it's a really bad idea to eat anything a fly's been sitting on!

DO FLIES TASTE WITH THEIR FEET?

Flies have 1,500 tiny taste hairs on their feet, so that they can taste what they are standing on.

DO FLIES LAY THEIR EGGS ON POOP?

The bluebottle and greenbottle flies common in houses lay their eggs in rotting meat, dead animals, and animal poop.

DID YOU KNOW?

A single female fly can hatch up to 1,000 babies (maggots) in her lifetime.

CAN YOU DIE FROM AN ANT STING?

The bulldog ant from Australia will sting again and again while holding on with its fierce jaws. It can kill a human in 15 minutes.

CAN ARMIES OF ANTS EAT LARGE PREY?

Driver ants and army ants both march in massive colonies and will strip to the bones any animal they come across. They'll even tackle a wounded crocodile or lion that can't get away. Driver ants slash at their victims, who eventually bleed to death from thousands of tiny cuts.

DID YOU KNOW?

The pharaoh ant likes to live in hospitals, where it feasts on wounds, bloody bandages, and IV solutions for dripping into patient's bodies.

HOW MUCH BLOOD DOES A LEECH DRINK?

A leech will suck blood until it is 10 times its original size and can't hold any longer. Once it's full, it drops off its victim. Leeches don't only suck from the outside of your body, either. If you drink water with a leech in it, the leech can attach to the inside of your mouth or throat. In a river, leeches can go into your bottom and suck you from the inside. Some leeches have three mouths, with up to 100 teeth.

WHY CAN'T YOU FEEL A LEECH BITING?

Many leeches produce a painkiller, so that you don't notice you've been bitten unless you actually see the leech.

DID YOU KNOW?

Some leeches can suck enough blood in one meal to keep them alive for nine months.

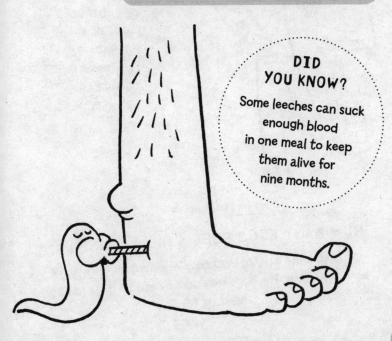

HOW HIGH CAN A FLEA JUMP?

A flea can jump 30,000 times without stopping. It can jump up to 220 times its own body length—a flea the size of an adult human could jump over a 25-floor building and 0.4 km (more than a quarter of a mile) along the ground.

HOW OFTEN DO HEAD LICE FEED?

Head lice suck blood for about 45 seconds every two to three hours, but they can go without a meal for up to two days if they are between heads—on a comb, towel, or pillow.

HOW MANY EGGS DOES A HEAD LOUSE LAY?

A head louse can lay 200 to 300 eggs during its life of about 30 days. The eggs only take five to 10 days to hatch and start feeding.

WHAT IS A PRAYING MANTIS?

A praying mantis is an insect something like a cricket but up to 12 cm (5 inches) long. It can kill and eat small lizards and birds, holding them impaled on a special spike it has developed for the purpose. The female praying mantis begins to eat the male during mating; he keeps going, but she eventually eats all of him.

DO ANY BUGS LAY THEIR EGGS ON DEAD ANIMALS?

When the necrophorus beetle finds a small dead animal, it pushes it into a suitable place, takes some of its fur to make a nest, and lays its eggs near the body. When the eggs hatch into maggots, they feed on the dead body.

DID YOU KNOW?

The potato beetle larva protects itself from birds that want to eat it by covering itself with its own poisonous poop.

IF YOU CUT A WORM IN HALF, WILL IT GROW AGAIN?

A planarian worm will regrow its other half if cut in two. If two planarians are cut in half, they can be mixed up and reattach to the wrong half.

DID YOU KNOW?

The job of guard termites is to defend the termite nest or mound. Sometimes they explode in their efforts to deter attackers.

WHICH CATERPILLAR GROWS THE FASTEST?

The caterpillar of the polyphemus moth in North America eats 86,000 times its own birth weight in the first 56 days of its life. This is equal to a human baby eating nearly 270 metric tons (600,000 lb) of food!

DO DUNG BEETLES EAT POOP?

African dung beetles eat animal poop. Five thousand beetles can eat 0.5 kg (1 lb) of poop in two hours.

DO TERMITES FART A LOT?

Termites fart out between 20 and 80 million metric tons of gas every year (not each— in total!).

WHAT ARE NOSE BOTS?

Nose bots are maggots that live inside the noses of animals that graze, such as sheep, cows, and horses.

DID YOU KNOW?

A ribbon worm can eat 95 % of its own body and still survive.

DID YOU KNOW?

Locusts such as giant grasshoppers or crickets, travel in swarms of up to 80 million, and each eats its own weight in plants every day.

WHAT ARE ZOMBIE WORMS?

Bone-eating zombie worms live on the decaying bodies of dead whales. They have no gut but bore deeply into the bones. Microbes inside the worms digest chemicals sucked out of the bones.

HOW DO YOU CATCH A SLUG?

Slugs are attracted to beer. Some gardeners trap them by putting out bowls of beer, which the slugs fall into. They get drunk and drown—the slugs, not the gardeners!

DID YOU KNOW?

The southern giant petrel, a bird that lives near the South Pole, spits globs of oil and regurgitated food at its enemies.

HORRID HISTORY

DO KINGS AND QUEENS GO TO THE TOILET?

Erm, yes. In France in the late 1600s, it was considered a great privilege to talk to King Louis XIV while he was on the toilet.

WHICH KING TRIED TO POISON HIMSELF?

Theban king Mithridates (132-63 BCE) took small doses of poison regularly to develop immunity and protect himself from poisoners. When he later wanted to kill himself, the poison he took didn't kill him.

WHY DID GREEK EMPEROR DRACO HATE PARTIES?

The Greek emperor Draco died when he was smothered by the hats and cloaks that admirers threw over him at a party.

WHY SHOULD YOU NEVER TELL TAMERLANE A JOKE?

Mongol leader Tamerlane the Great (1336-1405) executed anyone who told him a joke he had already heard. He also played polo using the skulls of enemies killed in battle.

WHO WAS THE SMELLIEST QUEEN?

Queen Isabella of Spain boasted that she only took two baths in her whole life—one when she was born and one before her wedding.

DID YOU KNOW?

Anyone who rebelled against the Mesopotamian king Ashurnasirpal could expect to be skinned or buried alive. We know this because he buried some rebels inside a column and carved the story of their crime on the outside.

WHY WAS ELIZABETH BATHORY THE BLOODY COUNTESS?

The Hungarian countess Elizabeth Bathory was one of the most fiendish people in history and liked to bathe in blood.

HOW DID QUEEN CHRISTINA STOP FLEAS?

Queen Christina of Sweden, who reigned from 1640 to 1654, had a miniature cannon and crossbow for executing fleas.

HOW DID IVAN THE TERRIBLE REWARD HIS ARCHITECTS?

Ivan the Terrible blinded the two architects who designed his new church of Saint Basil's, so that they could never make anything more beautiful.

WHAT DID PETER THE GREAT KEEP IN HIS MUSEUM?

Russian leader Peter the Great had a museum in which he kept the stuffed bodies of people and animals.

HOW DID KING URUKAGINA REMIND THIEVES OF THEIR CRIMES?

In 2350 BCE, the Mesopotamian king Urukagina demanded that thieves be stoned to death with stones carved with their crime.

WHY DID CHARLES THE FIRST LOSE AND FIND HIS HEAD AGAIN?

Charles I was executed by beheading but had his head sewed back on so that his family could pay their respects to his body. His doctor stole a bone from his neck and had it made into a saltshaker.

WHICH BRITISH KING WAS A POOR DINNER GUEST?

British king James I's tongue was too large for his mouth, so he slobbered all the time and was a very messy eater.

HOW DID VLAD THE IMPALER GET HIS NAME?

Vlad the Impaler, ruler of Transylvania, had over 20,000 enemies impaled on spikes between 1456 and 1476.

HOW DID IVAN THE TERRIBLE HOUND HIS ENEMIES?

Ivan the Terrible of Russia punished a bishop by having him stitched into the skin of a dead bear and releasing a pack of hounds to chase him.

WHAT DID KING WENCESLAS PUT ON THE MENU?

After a particularly bad meal, German king Wenceslas (1361-1419) was so angry that he had his chef killed.

WHICH KING RULED AFTER HE DIED?

King Kokodo of the Congo ruled for three years after his death. His body was wheeled around in a box during this part of his reign.

WHICH RULER WAS CROWNED IN HIS COFFIN?

Czar Peter III of Russia was crowned 34 years after he died. His coffin was opened, so that the crown could be put on his head.

WHICH KING HAS AN EXPLOSIVE END?

The body of William the Conqueror was too big for his coffin, so two soldiers jumped up and down on him to try to squish him in. This broke his back and made his stomach explode.

HOW COULD AMERICANS CLAIM THEIR OWN ISLAND?

In 1856, the United States passed a law saying that its citizens could claim any uninhabited island anywhere in the world if it contained large deposits of bird poop.

HOW DID THE GAME KNUCKLEBONES GET ITS NAME?

The Greeks played the game knucklebones with real bones from the knuckles of animals that have cloven feet, such as pigs, goats, and antelopes.

WHAT DID THE ANCIENT GREEKS USE FOR BALL GAMES?

Ancient Greeks used to blow up a pig's bladder like a balloon and use it as a ball.

DID FLEAS REALLY JOIN CIRCUSES?

In the 1800s, flea circuses were popular—the fleas were glued into costumes and stuck to wires or each other to look as though they were performing tricks.

DID YOU KNOW?

Scottish bagpipes were originally made from the entire skin or stomach of a dead sheep.

DID THE ROMANS REALLY MAKE PEOPLE FIGHT LIONS?

Yes. The Romans had criminals torn apart by wild animals while the public watched. Dogs or lions were most often used, but sometimes more exotic animals were brought in. Roman prisoners were condemned to fight to death with each other or wild animals.

HOW DID SLAVES AVOID A FIGHT TO THE DEATH?

Slaves sometimes had to fight to the death in a Roman arena. To make sure they weren't just pretending to be dead, they could be prodded with a red-hot poker and clonked on the head with a big hammer.

DID YOU KNOW?

The Roman king Tarquin crucified anyone who took their own life—even though they were already dead—to try to put other people off the idea.

WHAT WAS THE ROMAN CURE FOR BALDNESS?

Ancient Romans made hair dye from pigeon poop. Bald Romans used to make a paste of mashed-up flies and spread it over their heads in the belief that it would make their hair regrow. It didn't.

HOW DID THE ROMAN ARMY DEAL WITH DESERTERS?

In 167 BCE, a Roman commander had a group of soldiers trampled to death by elephants for deserting (running away from battle).

HOW DID ROMANS EAT SUCH BIG FEASTS?

Ancient Romans used to make themselves vomit during a banquet, so that they could eat more after they were full. A special slave had the job of cleaning up the mess.

HOW LONG DID IT TAKE TO MAKE A MUMMY?

It took over two months to make an Egyptian mummy. After removing the internal organs and brain, the body was covered with a kind of salt for two months to dry out, then treated with resin, packed with sand and sawdust, and wrapped in bandages. They used a special long-handled spoon to scoop the brains out through the dead person's nose. They often fed the brain to animals.

WHO WAS THE SCARIEST DINNER GUEST?

Ancient Egyptians sometimes brought a mummified body to banquets to remind diners that one day they would die.

WHY WAS IT BAD LUCK TO WORK FOR THE PHARAOH?

The servants of a dead Egyptian pharaoh were often killed and buried with him or sealed alive in his pyramid.

WAS THE TITANIC CURSED?

It is said that the cursed mummy of Egyptian princess Amen-Ra was on board the Titanic when it sank in 1912, killing 1,500 people. The mummy was being sent from the British Museum to the United States; only the lid of the mummy's coffin is still in the British Museum.

WHAT WAS THE ANCIENT EGYPTIAN CURE FOR BURNS?

An ancient Egyptian cure for burns involved warming a frog in goat dung and applying it to the burn.

HOW DID KING PEPI AVOID FLY BITES?

King Pepi II of Egypt had himself surrounded by naked slaves smeared with honey, so that any biting flies would be attracted to them and not bite him.

A common way of attacking a besieged castle or city in the Middle Ages was to catapult dead animals, corpses, or even the heads of enemies over the walls.

HOW DID A BOHEMIAN GENERAL INSPIRE HIS TROOPS AFTER DEATH?

A Bohemian army general was so devoted to his country that when he died, he asked for his skin to be removed and made into a drum that could be beaten in defiance of Bohemia's enemies. It was used nearly 200 years later at the start of the Thirty Years' War in 1618.

DID YOU KNOW?

Biological warfare has been used since 600 BCE when the Greek city Cirrha was besieged by Solon. He poisoned the water supply with hellebore roots and stormed the city while the citizens had the runs.

WHERE DID LORD NELSON SLEEP ABOARD SHIP?

Lord Nelson (1758-1805), admiral of the English fleet, slept in a coffin in his cabin. The coffin was made from the mast of an enemy French ship.

WHAT IS TRENCH FOOT?

Soldiers fighting in the trenches in World War I often suffered from trench foot (spending too long in cold, wet trenches made their feet rot). Some had to have their feet amputated because of it.

WHO FOUGHT OVER BIRD POOP?

In the War of the Pacific (1879-1884), Chile fought against Bolivia and Peru over who was allowed to collect bird poop and whether they should have to pay a tax on them.

DID YOU KNOW?

The Roman emperor Valerian was captured by Visigoths (a barbaric tribe) invading Rome in AD 260, who skinned him alive and then displayed the skin as a sign of their triumph.

WHAT DID 18TH-CENTURY PEOPLE WEAR ON THEIR HEADS?

In the 1700s, people wore huge hairstyles made of a mixture of human hair, horsehair, or other materials. Since they rarely cleaned them—keeping them in place for months on end—they carried sticks to knock vermin out of their hairdos.

WHY DID ANCIENT EGYPTIANS HAVE SHINY HAIR?

In ancient Egypt, women kept a cone of grease on their head. During the day, it melted in the hot sun and dripped down, making their hair gleam with grease.

WHAT DID WOMEN USE BEFORE LIPSTICK?

Before the days of lipstick, women used to paint their lips red with cochineal, a paste made from crushed beetles.

HOW DID KING CHARLES BOOST WOOL SALES?

In the time of King Charles II of England, who reigned from 1649 to 1685, dead people had to be buried in a shroud made of wool to boost business for the wool trade.

WHAT IS A FULLER?

Wool used to be softened by people trampling on it in a large vat of stale (two-week-old) urine and ground clay. The people who did this were called "fullers."

DID YOU KNOW?

Inuit people used to make pants (or trousers) out of the gullet (windpipe) of a seal or walrus, using one for each leg.

DID YOU KNOW?

Anglo-Saxon peasants sometimes wove clothes made out of dried stinging nettles.

HOW DID 19TH-CENTURY WOMEN LOOK SO THIN?

In the 1890s, fashionable women in Europe who wanted to look thin wore corsets laced so tightly that their ribs were sometimes broken!

WHAT DID 18TH-CENTURY WOMEN USE FOR EYEBROWS?

In the 1700s, fashionable European women commonly shaved off their real eyebrows and stuck on false ones made from mouse fur.

WHY DID 18TH-CENTURY WOMEN PIERCE THEIR GUMS?

In the 1700s, European women had their gums pierced, so that they could fit hooks to hold their false teeth in place.

DID YOU KNOW?

Fashionable women in Japan and Vietnam stained their teeth black until the mid-1900s.

WHAT WAS LIFE LIKE FOR A CHIMNEY SWEEP?

Victorian child chimney sweeps sometimes had to crawl through chimneys as narrow as 18 cm (7 inches). If they didn't go quickly enough, their bare feet were pricked with burning straws. The sweeps used to take three baths a year—one in the spring, one in the autumn, and one for Christmas. The rest of the time, they were covered in soot.

HOW DID ANCIENT EGYPTIANS CATCH FLEAS?

In ancient Egypt, a flea catcher would cover himself in milk and stand in the middle of a flea-infested room until all the fleas jumped on to him. Then he'd leave, taking them all with him.

HOW DID YOU AMUSE A MEDIEVAL KING?

In the Middle Ages a royal farter was employed to jump around farting in front of the king to make him laugh.

HOW DID PRINCES AVOID PUNISHMENT?

In the old days, a "whipping boy" used to sit next to a prince during lessons. If the prince made a mistake or did something wrong, the whipping boy was punished instead of the prince.

WHAT WAS A GONG SCOURER?

Before modern plumbing, a gong scourer was a boy who was sent into cesspits to scoop and scrape all the muck into buckets and remove it. The job was so horrible, it was done at night so that people wouldn't have to see it happening.

DID YOU KNOW?

Girls who made matches in the 1800s often suffered from "phossy jaw"——their jawbones would rot away, poisoned by the phosphorus used to make the matches.

HOW DID TOADS SELL MEDICINE?

Toadeaters were people employed by men selling medicine at fairs and markets. The toadeater had to swallow a toad— supposed to be deadly poisonous— and then take the medicine. Their survival encouraged people to buy the medicine. They may or may not have actually swallowed the toads ...

HOW DID SAXONS PREVENT MADNESS?

A Saxon cure for madness was a beating with a whip made from the skin of a dolphin.

HOW DID ANGLO SAXONS CURE BALDNESS?

An Anglo-Saxon cure for baldness was to rub the ash from burned bees into the head.

WHY SHOULD YOU NEVER TRY ANCIENT EGYPTIAN MEDICINE?

An ancient Egyptian who was feeling a bit unwell might eat a mixture of mashed mouse and poop. Yum! Bound to make you feel better!

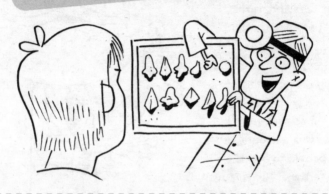

WHAT WAS THE FIRST COSMETIC SURGERY?

The earliest cosmetic surgery was done by doctors in India, who made fake noses for criminals whose noses had been cut off as a punishment for their crimes.

DID YOU KNOW?

In the 1600s and later, Egyptian mummies were ground up to use in medicines around Europe.

WHY WAS IT SAFER TO BE IN PRISON IN 1577?

In 1577, an outbreak of typhus in a jail in Oxford, England, killed 300 people——the judges, jury, witnesses, and spectators at criminal trials. The prisoners, used to living in filthy conditions, all survived.

WHY WERE INNOCENT PEOPLE BURNED IN THE MIDDLE AGES?

A medieval trial of guilt required a suspected criminal to plunge his or her hand into a pan of hot water and take out a stone, or carry a red-hot iron bar. The injured arm was bandaged and inspected after three days. If it was healed, the person was considered innocent. If not, they were guilty and were punished.

WHY WAS PEEING DEADLY IN MONGOLIA?

The Mongolian ruler Genghis Khan imposed the death penalty for peeing in water because water was so precious in the Mongolian desert.

DID YOU KNOW?

In 1740, a cow found guilty of witchcraft was hanged.

HOW WAS A GOAT USED AS PUNISHMENT?

A French medieval torture involved trapping a person in the stocks—a wooden structure that held their ankles while they sat on the ground—pouring salt water over their bare feet, and letting a goat lick it off.

DID YOU KNOW?

In 1685, a wolf that terrorized a village near Ansbach in Germany was sentenced to be dressed in human clothing and hanged.

WHAT WAS THE SPANISH INQUISITION?

The Spanish Inquisition was set up to find people who committed crimes against the church and its teachings. They often questioned and tortured people until they confessed.

WHAT WAS THE NASTIEST PUNISHMENT IN 13TH-CENTURY ENGLAND?

Hanging, drawing, and quartering was a punishment for the worst crimes in England from 1241. First, the prisoner was hanged until almost dead, then cut open, had his innards removed and cooked in front of him, and finally, was chopped into four pieces. By the mid-1700s, prisoners were killed before the drawing and quartering stages.

WHEN WAS A TRIP TO AUSTRALIA NOT FUN?

Until 1868, criminals could be transported from England and sent to Australia for 7-14 years as punishment for even petty crimes. The youngest victim was a boy of nine who was transported for stealing.

DID YOU KNOW?

Romans who killed a relative would be executed by being tied in a sack with a live dog, rooster, snake, and monkey and thrown into a river.

HOW COULD YOU SPOT A CRIMINAL IN THE DISTANT PAST?

Before written or computerized records helped us keep track of criminals, many countries marked criminals with a tattoo or a branding iron—a red-hot iron used to burn a pattern, letter, or picture into their skin. This meant that everyone could see what they had done.

WHAT WAS A GIBBET?

Long ago, criminals would be hanged in a metal cage called a gibbet, or in chains, near the scene of their crime until their bones rotted to nothing.

WERE DOGS EVER SENT TO PRISON?

A Lhasa apso dog was once imprisoned and kept on death row in a prison in Washington State for over eight years—for biting.

DID YOU KNOW?

In the 1700s, the penalty for wearing tartan or playing the bagpipes in Britain was death.

WHERE WERE THE DEAD BURIED 8,000 YEARS AGO?

In Palestine 8,000–9,000 years ago, dead relatives were buried under the floor of a family's house—except the head. The flesh and brains were removed from the head and the skull used as the base for a plaster model of the person's head, which was decorated and kept.

WERE THERE CANNIBALS IN ANGLO-SAXON TIMES?

In Anglo-Saxon England, people who died in a famine were eaten by locals!

HOW DID SIR WALTER RALEIGH'S WIFE REMEMBER HIM?

When Sir Walter Raleigh was executed in 1618, his wife had his head embalmed. She carried it around with her for 29 years, until her own death.

WHAT DID THE POET SHELLEY LEAVE FOR HIS WIFE?

The poet Shelley drowned off the coast of Italy in 1822. His body was washed up, half eaten by fish, and cremated on the beach by his friends. One of them cut his heart from the burned body and gave it to Shelley's wife, who kept it all her life.

WHERE CAN YOU SEE 6,000 MUMMIES?

Monks in Sicily, Italy, mummified dead bodies until 1920. A display of 6,000 of them can be seen in catacombs in Palermo, standing around or lying on shelves.

DID YOU KNOW?

The Incas of South America used to mummify their dead kings and leave them sitting on their thrones.

HOW DID SAILORS PAY FOR THEIR FUNERALS?

Sailors in the olden days often had a single gold tooth, which could be pulled out and used to pay for their funeral if they died away from home.

HOW DID A RUGBY TEAM SURVIVE 70 DAYS LOST IN THE ANDES?

Uruguay's rugby team was stranded in the Andes in South America after a plane crash in 1979. It took 70 days for them to be rescued, and they had to eat the other passengers who had died in the crash.

DID YOU KNOW?

A dead body found in the Alps in 1991 was at first thought to be a climber who had died. Investigators discovered it was a man who had been mummified naturally in the ice after dying 5,300 years ago. They named him Otzi.

WHERE CAN YOU SEE A 270-YEAR-OLD BODY?

The body of British philosopher Jeremy Bentham (1748–1832) was preserved and kept in an open wooden box, which is still on display at University College, London. For many years, Bentham was brought out to attend special functions and meetings.

WHO WAS HAPPY TO BE EATEN BY LIONS?

Saint Ignatius of Antioch prayed to be eaten by wild animals; when the Roman emperor Trajan sentenced him to be eaten by lions in 110, he fell to his knees and thanked him.

HOW DO YOU PAINT A DEAD DUKE?

James, Duke of Monmouth, was beheaded in 1685, but when it was discovered that there was no official portrait of him, his head was stitched back on and he posed for his portrait at last.

WHICH POPE WENT ON TRIAL AFTER DEATH?

In 896, the rotting body of Pope Formosus was removed from his coffin, dressed in his papal robes, and put on trial. Found guilty, his blessing finger was cut off, and he was thrown in the river.

WHICH QUEEN REFUSED TO LOSE HER HEAD?

It took the executioner three blows to behead Mary, Queen of Scots, in 1567.

WHAT DID SPECTATORS TAKE HOME FROM BEHEADINGS?

During the French Revolution, large crowds watched public executions by guillotine, and people would rush forward to try to collect blood dripping from the heads lifted to show the crowd. They would keep bloody handkerchiefs as souvenirs of the outing. During the Reign of Terror following the French Revolution, 17,000 people were beheaded using the guillotine.

WAS ANYONE EVER BURIED BY MISTAKE?

In the 1800s, there were several cases of people being buried when they were not really dead. Terrible stories about opened coffins with scratch marks on the inside and corpses with fingernails worn away by trying to escape led to cautious people being buried with a system of warning bells fitted in the coffin, which they could ring if they woke up.

DID YOU KNOW?

English revolutionary Oliver Cromwell died of natural causes, but opponents had his body dug up, tried, and executed. His head is kept in an unmarked location in Sidney Sussex College, Cambridge, UK.

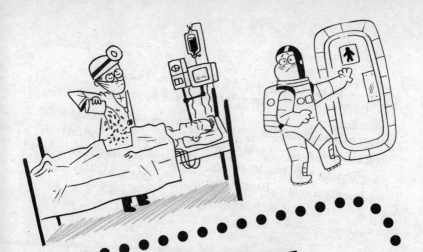

SCARY
SCIENCE

HOW WERE HEADACHES CURED IN THE STONE AGE?

Many tribes around the world have performed trepanning since the Stone Age. It involves drilling a hole in the skull, often with a stone, to ease headaches by letting out evil spirits. People frequently survived, because many skulls have been found with several such holes, some partially healed.

HOW WERE ANTS USED IN SURGERY?

Early Indian surgeons used ants to hold the edges of wounds together. They would get an ant to bite through both sides of the wound, then twist off the ant's body and throw it away, leaving the head in place with the jaws acting as a stitch.

DID YOU KNOW?

A cure for whooping cough used in Yorkshire, England, in the 1800s was to drink a bowl of soup with nine frogs hidden in it. You couldn't make it yourself—it only worked if you didn't know about the frogs. (And probably not then, either!)

HOW DID A BULLET WOUND HELP A DOCTOR'S STUDIES?

In 1822, Dr. William Beaumont studied human digestion as it happened, through a hole in the side and stomach of a patient who had been shot. The hole didn't heal, allowing Dr. Beaumont to study, but also allowing food and drink to ooze out if it wasn't covered up.

WHAT IS MALARIA?

Malaria is a deadly disease spread by mosquitoes. It's caused by a tiny parasite that lives inside a person's blood cells. Malaria kills up to three million people a year.

DID YOU KNOW?

In an attempt to kill malaria-carrying mosquitoes, an American scientist built towers to attract bats. He enticed them in with fabric covered with bat droppings and played music near the bats' old homes to drive them out. After a few years, malaria infection dropped from 89 percent of the population to zero.

HOW DID GOLDFISH SAVE LIVES IN WWI?

During World War I, goldfish were used to check whether all traces of poisonous gas had been washed out of gas masks. The mask was rinsed and filled with water, then a goldfish was dropped in. If it died, there was still gas left in it.

DID YOU KNOW?

Horses killed in World War I were recycled as explosives——their fat was removed and boiled down to be used in making TNT.

HOW DO RATS FIND LANDMINES?

Rats trained to look for land mines are so light that they don't trigger the mechanism if they step on one. Instead, they scratch and bite at the ground when they smell explosives, and the handler deals with the mine.

CAN POTATOES KILL YOU?

Green potatoes contain a poison, solanine, which can be deadly. It develops in old potatoes that aren't kept in the dark. Eating 2 kg (4.4 lb) of green potatoes could be fatal.

DID YOU KNOW?

Taking a bath in the water used to wash a corpse was thought to cure epilepsy.

WHEN IS HONEY DEADLY?

A toxin in the nectar of laurels and rhododendrons causes honey made from these plants to be poisonous. In 66 BCE, Roman troops were lured by their enemies into a grove where bees made honey from these flowers. The soldiers ate it and were slaughtered while sick.

HOW CAN FIREFLIES HELP SCIENTISTS?

Scientists investigating abnormal lumps added a gene from a firefly to make a glow-in-the-dark lump. The lump is visible through the skin of a test animal, so scientists can see if it grows or shrinks.

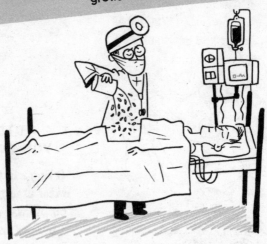

HOW CAN MAGGOTS HELP SURGEONS?

One of the best ways of cleaning an infected wound is to put maggots into it to eat the rotting flesh. This was used before the days of antibiotics and now with infections that antibiotics can't treat.

HOW CAN YOU TELL THE AGE OF A DEAD BODY?

Police scientists investigating a murder can tell how long a body has been dead by looking at the kinds of maggots, worms, and insects that are eating it.

WHICH ANIMALS WERE USED TO DETECT GAS?

Some animals respond to small amounts of poisonous gas and have been used as early warning systems. German soldiers kept cats in the trenches of World War I to smell gas, and British miners kept budgies in cages because they died quickly if gas escaped into the mine.

COULD BLUE WHALES LIVE ON LAND?

If blue whales tried to live on land, they would be crushed and suffocated by their own weight. They can live successfully in water because it supports them.

HOW LONG DOES IT TAKE A DEAD WHALE TO DISAPPEAR?

It can take 100 years for the body of a whale at the bottom of the sea to disappear completely as it is slowly eaten away by different animals, plants, and microbes.

CAN A MOUSE SURVIVE A FALL FROM A GREAT HEIGHT?

A small animal such as a mouse can be dropped 1,000 m (3,280 ft) down a mine shaft and suffer no harm because the fastest speed it can fall is not enough to crush its body.

The larger an animal or object, the shorter the distance it can safely fall.

WHY IS BLOOD RED?

Our blood is red because it uses an iron compound to carry oxygen—some spiders have blue blood because theirs uses a copper compound instead.

DID YOU KNOW?

Scraping rotten parts off your food doesn't get rid of them—behind the fuzzy parts you can see, strings extend into the food up to nine times the length of the visible areas.

HOW MUCH EARTH DO WORMS MOVE?

Earthworms bring 4 million kg (8.8 million lb) of earth to the surface on every square km (0.38 square mile) of open ground each year.

WHAT WAS THE ANCESTOR OF ALL VERTEBRATES?

Scientists believe that all vertebrates (animals with backbones) evolved from giant tadpoles, 2.5 inches (6 cm) long, that swam around 550 million years ago.

DID YOU KNOW?

There are 100 million times more insects than people on Earth, and their total weight is 12 times the total weight of people.

WHY ARE SOME DEAD BODIES FROZEN?

Some wealthy people have their bodies cryopreserved (deep-frozen) when they die in the hope that in the future, someone will find a cure for their cause of death and resurrect them. The popular urban legend that Walt Disney was cryopreserved is false: He was cremated.

WHAT'S THE BIGGEST LIVING THING IN THE WORLD?

The largest living thing in the world is a fungus in Washington State, which covers 6.5 square km (2.5 square miles) and has been growing for hundreds of years.

DID YOU KNOW?

The average bed is home to 6 million dust mites.

WHAT'S THE DEADLIEST NATURAL POISON?

The castor bean plant contains the most deadly poison in the natural world, ricin. Just 70 micrograms (two-millionths of an ounce) could kill an adult human. It's 12,000 times more poisonous than rattlesnake venom!

WHY SHOULD YOU FEAR A WILL-O'-THE-WISP?

A will-o'-the-wisp is a flame of burning marsh gas that appears in boggy areas at night. It has lured many wanderers to a muddy death when they left the path to follow it, believing it to be someone with a light.

DID YOU KNOW?

It's said that dead Americans rot much more slowly than they used to—because they eat so many preservatives in their foods.

WHAT'S THE SMELLIEST PLANT?

The stinking corpse plant, or rafflesia, is a huge parasitic flower that smells like rotting meat. The flower is about 1 m (3 ft) across and is the largest flower in the world. It grows directly out of a creeping vine, from which it gains all its nourishment without ever growing leaves of its own.

HOW FAST DOES BACTERIA REPRODUCE?

Bacteria—tiny living things that we also call germs—divide in two every 20 minutes. So, starting with one (it doesn't need a girlfriend/boyfriend), you can have over 130 million in just nine hours!

DID YOU KNOW?

Lined up neatly, 10,000 bacteria would stretch across your thumbnail.

WHY DID SURGEONS BUY DEAD BODIES?

For centuries, it was illegal to cut up dead bodies, so surgeons and scientists had to pay criminals to steal the corpses of executed prisoners from the gallows in order to learn about anatomy.

HOW DO SCABS FORM?

Scabs are formed when chemical proteins react with special blood cells called platelets, which cause the cells to get sticky and clump together. Once they've clotted, lots of different chemicals and cells work together to dry out the clot and form a scab, keeping out germs while the cells underneath repair themselves. So if you pick a scab, you're tampering with all your body's hard work!

DID YOU KNOW?

The average glass of London tap water has passed through nine people's bladders before it reaches the sink.

WHO INVENTED THE FROZEN CHICKEN?

The first frozen chicken was created by Sir Francis Bacon, who stuffed a plucked chicken with snow in 1626 to experiment with refrigeration. It worked, but he died from a chill contracted during the experiment. The chicken is said to haunt Pond Square in London, England.

HOW CAN MUSEUMS USE BEETLES?

Dermestid beetles are so good at stripping the flesh off dead animals that natural history museums use their larvae to clean up skeletons they are going to put on display.

DID YOU KNOW?

In 2000, UK mountaineer Major Michael Lane gave a museum five of his own fingers and eight of his toes, which had dropped off as a result of frostbite when he was climbing Mount Everest in 1976.

WHAT'S THE MOST POISONOUS METAL?

The most poisonous metal in the world is arsenic. It used to be made into flypaper for killing flies, but it killed some people, too.

HOW DID FACE PAINT CAUSE DEATH?

In the past, people used white lead powder to make their skin look white, but it gave them lead poisoning and slowly killed them. Since their skin looked worse once the poison took effect, they used more white lead to cover up the damage.

HOW DO DEODORANTS WORK?

Deodorants don't stop you from sweating, but they kill the bacteria that make sweat smell.

WHY DID ENGINEERS BUILD A ROBOT KANGAROO?

There are over 20,000 road crashes involving kangaroos in Australia every year, so a robotic, kangaroo-like crash-test dummy called Robo-Roo is used to test how badly cars will be damaged.

WHY DESIGN A ROBOT TADPOLE?

Scientists are working on a microscopic robotic tadpole to deliver medicines—the tadpole will "swim" through the patient's blood vessels to take the medicine where it's needed.

DID YOU KNOW?

Diamonds are so hard, they are often used as the tip of a dentist's drill because they can grind through teeth.

WHAT IS OIL MADE FROM?

Oil is made from the decayed bodies of animals and plants that died millions of years ago and have been squashed deep underground.

WHAT WILL WE DO WHEN WE RUN OUT OF OIL?

Among fuels investigated for use where (or when) oil and gas are scarce, scientists have tried running cars and tractors on chicken poop.

CAN YOU DROWN IN MUD?

It's possible to drown in mud—but really unlikely. If someone was drowning in mud, it would be almost impossible to save them since so much force is needed to pull them against the weight of it.

HOW BIG ARE BACTERIA?

Most bacteria are only about 0.00025 of a cm (0.0001 of an inch) across. But monster bacteria have been found at the bottom of the ocean off the coast of Africa. They are so big, they can be seen without a microscope— they're each about the size of a pencil dot.

WHAT WOULD HAPPEN IF YOU FELL INTO A BLACK HOLE?

If you fell into a black hole, you would be stretched into an incredibly long, thin string in a process called "spaghettification."

WHAT IS IT LIKE TO PEE IN SPACE?

It is so cold in space, that pee flushed out of a spacecraft instantly freezes into a stream of yellow crystals.